STEM Superstars

Steven Hawking

by Michelle Parkin

NorwoodHouse Press

Cover: Stephen Hawking was one of the world's most important scientists.

Norwood House Press
For information regarding Norwood House Press, please visit our website at: www.norwoodhousepress.com or call 866-565-2900.

PHOTO CREDITS: Cover, ©Samir Hussein / Contributor / Getty Images; 5, ©S-F/ Shutterstock; 6, ©Tony Rowell/Getty Images; 9, ©Thana Prasongsin/Getty Images; 11, ©Atlantic Productions / SKY Studios / Album/Newscom; 13, ©Mirrorpix / Contributor/ Getty Images; 14, ©Mike Marsland / Contributor/Getty Images; 17, ©Helen Dream/ Shutterstock; 18, ©Ralph Orlowski / Staff/Getty Images; 21, ©Ralph Orlowski / Staff/ Getty Images

Hardcover ISBN: 978-1-68450-742-9
Paperback ISBN: 978-1-68404-824-3

© 2023 by Norwood House Press.

All rights reserved.

No part of this book may be reproduced without written permission from the publisher.

Library of Congress Cataloging-in-Publication Data

Names: Parkin, Michelle, 1984- author.
Title: Stephen Hawking / by Michelle Parkin.
Description: [Chicago] : Norwood House Press, [2023] | Series: Stem superstars | Includes index. | Audience: Ages 5-8 | Audience: Grades K-1 | Summary: "Describes the life and work of Stephen Hawking, a physicist who developed theories on black holes and the formation of the universe"-- Provided by publisher.
Identifiers: LCCN 2022037297 (print) | LCCN 2022037298 (ebook) | ISBN 9781684507429 (hardcover) | ISBN 9781684048243 (paperback) | ISBN 9781684048441 (ebook)
Subjects: LCSH: Hawking, Stephen, 1942-2018--Juvenile literature. | Physicists--Great Britain--Biography--Juvenile literature. | Amyotrophic lateral sclerosis--Patients--Great Britain--Biography--Juvenile literature.
Classification: LCC QC16.H33 P368 2023 (print) | LCC QC16.H33 (ebook) | DDC 530.092 [B]--dc23/eng/20220809
LC record available at https://lccn.loc.gov/2022037297
LC ebook record available at https://lccn.loc.gov/2022037298

359N–012023
Manufactured in the United States of America in North Mankato, Minnesota.

Table of Contents

Chapter 1
Early Life..................................4

Chapter 2
Star Studies............................10

Chapter 3
Famous Scientist 16

Career Connections 22
Glossary 23
For More Information 23
Index 24
About the Author 24

Chapter 1

Early Life

Stephen Hawking was born on January 8, 1942. He was from Oxford, England. Education was important to his family. Everyone read books. They even read at the dinner table.

In Oxford, Hawking grew up with three siblings.

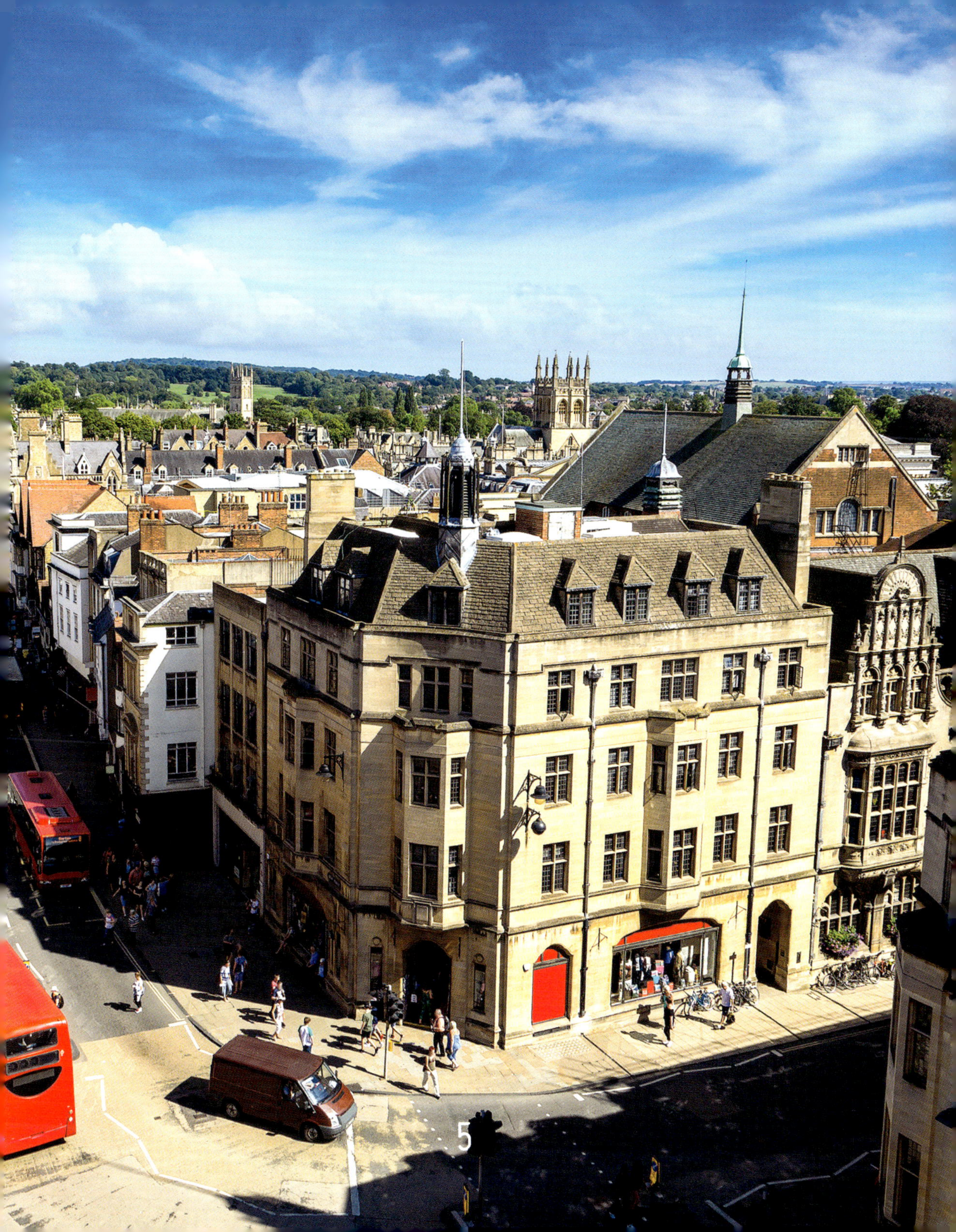

Hawking loved to learn about outer space.

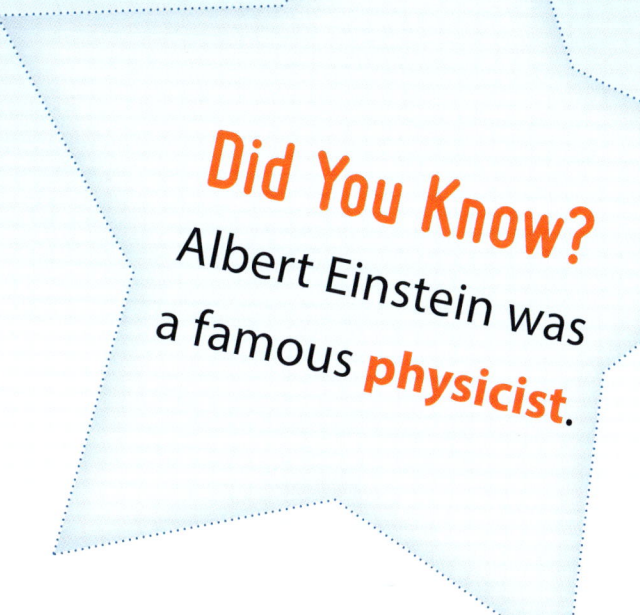

> **Did You Know?**
> Albert Einstein was a famous **physicist**.

Hawking did not do well in school. But he liked science. He built amazing things. He used items people threw away. His friends called him Einstein.

Did You Know?

A teacher inspired Hawking to study science and math in college.

Once, Hawking built a computer. He used old clock parts. He added parts from a telephone. The computer worked.

⭐ **Computers and other technology were a big part of Hawking's life.**

Chapter 2

Star Studies

Hawking went to college. He was only 17. The school was University College in Oxford. Hawking studied **physics**. This time, he did well in school. Later, he went to the University of Cambridge. He studied outer space.

⭐ Hawking's parents wanted him to be a doctor.

11

Did You Know?
There is no cure for ALS.

Hawking found out he had **ALS**. He was 21. ALS is a deadly illness. The brain cannot **communicate** with the body.

Doctors said Hawking would live for two more years. He lived another 55 years!

A movie about Hawking came out in 2014.

Did You Know?
Hawking liked to drive his wheelchair fast. He would run over people's toes!

People with ALS have trouble walking. Talking and swallowing are also hard. Hawking had to use a walking stick. Later, he used a wheelchair.

Chapter 3

Famous Scientist

Hawking lived with ALS. He still became one of the greatest scientists of all time. He is most famous for his work on **black holes**. He explained what they are. He taught people how they are made.

⭐ **The first picture of a black hole was taken in 2019.**

17

Hawking wrote about how the universe formed.

Did You Know?
Hawking also wrote children's science books with his daughter.

    Hawking wanted everyone to understand his ideas. He wrote over 20 books. One book became very popular. It is called *A Brief History of Time*. It sold over 10 million copies.

Did You Know?
Hawking used a special computer to talk.

Hawking died on March 14, 2018. Today, scientists still use his ideas in their work.

⭐ **Hawking encouraged others to never give up.**

21

★ Career Connections ★

1. Astronomers study space. They map out the stars. You can too! Look at the stars at night. Draw a picture of what you see.

2. Hawking loved to read. There are many careers for people who love to read. Librarians, editors, and archivists all work with books. Get a jump start on a reading career. Ask an adult to help you get your own library card at your local library.

3. Hawking recycled! He used thrown-out items to make new things. Look around for items you are not using anymore. Use glue or string and make something new.

4. Imagine you are a great scientist. What type of scientist would you be? Learn more about that career. Ask an adult for help getting started.

5. Learn about other scientists. What did they study in school? What kinds of jobs did they have?

★ Glossary ★

ALS (ay-el-ESS): ALS stands for amyotrophic lateral sclerosis. ALS is a disease. It affects the brain and spine. This causes the loss of muscle control over time.

black holes (BLAK HOLHZ): Areas in space where gravity pulls so hard that even light cannot get out.

communicate (kuh-MYOO-nuh-kate): To share information.

physicist (FIZ-uh-sist): A person who studies how matter and energy behave.

physics (FIZ-iks): The science that deals with matter and energy. It includes the study of light, heat, sound, electricity, motion, and force.

★ For More Information ★

Books

Betts, Bruce. *Super Cool Space Facts: A Fun, Fact-Filled Space Book for Kids*. Emeryville, CA: Rockridge Press, 2019. Learn facts about stars, planets, black holes, and more.

Castro, Rachel. *Mae Jemison*. STEM Superstars. Chicago, IL: Norwood House Press, 2020. Read this book to learn about another famous person who loves space, Mae Jemison.

Websites

10 Facts About Stephen Hawking
(www.natgeokids.com/uk/discover/science/general-science/stephen-hawking-facts/) Learn fun facts about Stephen Hawking.

NASA Kids' Club
(https://www.nasa.gov/kidsclub/index.html) Learn about space, planets, and more on this NASA website.

★ Index ★

A

A Brief History of Time, 19

ALS, 12, 15, 16

B

black holes, 16

C

computer, 8, 20

O

Oxford, England, 4, 10

S

science, 7–8, 19

U

University College, 10

University of Cambridge, 10

★ About the Author ★

Michelle Parkin is an editor and a children's book author. She has written more than 15 children's books about famous people, animals, and dinosaurs. She lives with her daughter and golden retriever mix in Minnesota.